THIS BOOK BELONGS TO

_____

Jesus Teaches Me

Parables for Children

Written by Randy-Lynne Wach
Illustrated by Jerry Harston

DESERET
BOOK

To my little princesses,
who inspire me to always try harder
—R-LW

With love to my sixteen grandchildren
—JH

Library of Congress Cataloging-in-Publication Data
Wach, Randy-Lynne.
  Jesus teaches me : parables for children / Randy-Lynne Wach ; illustrated by Jerry Harston.
    p. cm.
  ISBN-13: 978-1-59038-724-5 (hardbound : alk. paper)
  1. Jesus Christ—Parables—Juvenile literature. I. Harston, Jerry. II. Title.
  BT376.W33 2007
  226.8'09505—dc22   2006033204

Printed in Mexico
R. R. Donnelley and Sons, Reynosa, Mexico
10   9   8   7   6   5   4   3   2   1

Contents

Jesus Teaches Me to Be Kind to Others

Jesus Teaches Me to Pray

Jesus Teaches Me to Repent

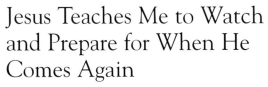

Jesus Teaches Me to Choose the Right

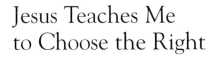

Jesus Teaches Me to Watch and Prepare for When He Comes Again

When Jesus was on the earth,
He told stories called parables. Jesus told parables
to explain how to live the gospel.
When I read His words in the scriptures,
Jesus can teach me, too.

Jesus Teaches Me to Love the Gospel

The Pearl of Great Price (Matthew 13:45–46)

There was a merchant who went all over the world looking for beautiful pearls. One day he found a pearl, large and round and perfect. He had seen many beautiful pearls, but knew this pearl was more rare and valuable than all the others. If he searched the rest of his life, he would never find a pearl as special as this one.

He happily sold everything he owned, including many other lovely pearls, in order to buy that one perfect pearl.

The gospel of Jesus Christ is perfect, more precious than anything else in this world. Am I willing to give up everything I have to follow Jesus and keep His commandments?

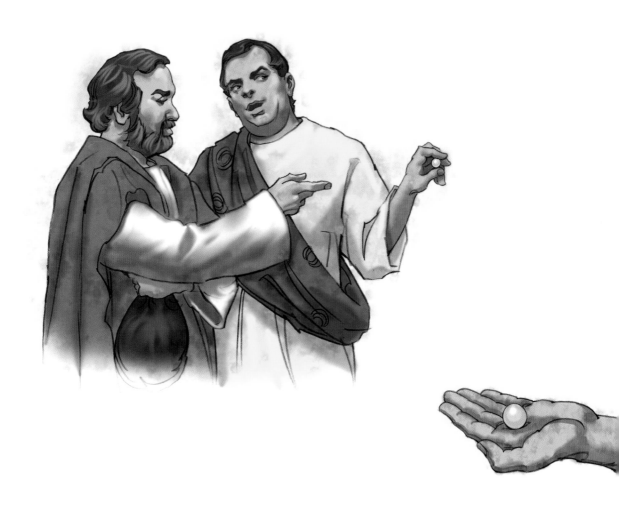

The Hidden Treasure (Matthew 13:44)

While walking through a field, a man found a hidden treasure. He quickly sold everything he had and used the money to buy the field. He was happy because the treasure was now his!

I am lucky to have found Jesus' teachings. I can keep His commandments. I can obey my mom and dad, go to church, and be nice to others. When I do these things, it makes me happy.

The Foolish Rich Man (Luke 12:16–21)

There was a man who worked very hard. He was successful and made lots of money. With the money, he bought many expensive things.

One day, he realized he had so much, he didn't have a place to keep it all. So he tore down his old house and built a great mansion. Then he piled it high with all his belongings. He told himself that he didn't have to work so hard anymore. He had enough to last for many years.

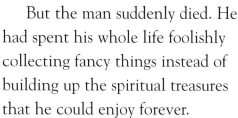

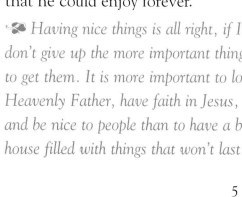

But the man suddenly died. He had spent his whole life foolishly collecting fancy things instead of building up the spiritual treasures that he could enjoy forever.

Having nice things is all right, if I don't give up the more important things to get them. It is more important to love Heavenly Father, have faith in Jesus, and be nice to people than to have a big house filled with things that won't last.

5

Jesus Teaches Me How to Get a Strong Testimony

The Sower and the Soils (Matthew 13:3–9, 19–23; Mark 4:3–8; Luke 8:5–8)

A long time ago, farmers would scatter seeds to plant their fields. When it was time to plant, the farmer would throw the seeds into the air, and the wind would carry the seeds around the field.

Some seeds would fall onto pathways where people would step on them and crush them. Birds would also come and eat them up. Those seeds never had a chance to grow.

Some seeds would fall into rocky places, and plants would start to grow. But the sun was too hot for them because the roots couldn't get past the rocks to reach water. So those plants wilted and died.

Some seeds would fall into patches of weeds. They would sprout, but the weeds would steal all the water and nourishment from the ground. Those tender plants didn't have the strength they needed to flower and bear fruit.

But some seeds would fall into good, rich soil. There they were able to send down deep roots. Those plants grew and flowered and bore fruit. Some made a little fruit, some made a lot of fruit, and some made even more.

 *For a testimony to grow, it has to take root in good soil. The soil in this parable is like my heart. My heart needs to be soft and open so that I will love Jesus, so that I will want to obey His commandments, and so that I will believe what my mom and dad and the scriptures teach me. What can I do to open my heart to Heavenly Father's teachings?*

Jesus Teaches Me to Share the Gospel

The Hidden Candle (Mark 4:21–22; Luke 8:16–18)

A candle does no good if it's covered up or hidden under the table. Candles are placed high, in the middle of the room, to provide light for as much of the room as possible. That way everyone in the room can see.

The gospel is for everyone, not for just a few people. I need to share my testimony with others. What are the ways I can share the gospel light with my friends?

The Leaven (Matthew 13:33; Luke 13:20–21)

Leaven is like yeast. It is used to make bread light and fluffy instead of hard and flat. While baking bread, a woman mixed a little leaven into a batch of dough. The leaven soon spread through the batch, making the whole loaf rise.

Even though I am young, I have been taught the gospel, and there are things I can do to share the gospel message with my friends—I can be a good example, invite them to church, and be kind. Just like leaven, my testimony can spread.

The Mustard Seed (Matthew 13:31–32; Mark 4:30–32; Luke 13:18–19)

A man planted a tiny mustard seed in his garden. Soon that tiny seed grew into a tall bush. The bush was so tall, the birds thought it was a tree and built their nests in it.

Like the tiny mustard seed, the Church started small, with just a few good people. But as more and more people heard the gospel, the Church grew. What are some of the things I can do to help more people learn about the gospel?

Jesus Teaches Me to Use My Talents

The Talents (Matthew 25:14–30; Luke 19:11–26)

A man decided to take a trip. He knew he would be gone for a long time, so he left three of his servants in charge of his things. He gave one man five talents (a kind of money), another man two, and just one talent to the third man. Then he left.

The first servant took his five talents and traded with them. He chose carefully where he put the money, and made five more talents.

The next servant did the same, making two more talents.

The last servant was afraid he might lose the money if he tried to trade with it, and he buried it in the ground so it would be safe.

When the man came back from his trip, he wanted to know how well his money had been taken care of. So he called the three servants to him.

The first said, "Look. You gave me five talents, and now I have ten."

The man was happy and said, "Well done. You have used a little money well. Now I know I can trust you with even more."

The second said, "See, I now have four talents, where you gave me only two." And the second man was also rewarded.

The third servant said, "I was afraid you would get mad if I lost the talent, and I buried it so I could give it back to you." He then returned the talent to its owner.

The owner was unhappy with the third servant and said, "That was very foolish. Now I have nothing more than what I started with. If you had at least put it into a bank it would have made some interest." He then gave the one talent to the servant with ten. The foolish servant was sent away, since he could not be trusted to care for even a little.

Heavenly Father has blessed me with special abilities. If I don't use them, I may lose what I already have. What are my special talents? What can I do to multiply them? How can I use my talents to bless other people?

Jesus Teaches Me to Follow the Prophet

The Rich Man and Lazarus (Luke 16:19–31)

Once there was a rich man who dressed in fancy clothes and had plenty to eat every day. At the same time there was a beggar named Lazarus. Lazarus was always hungry, and he would fight with the dogs for the scraps of food left over after the rich man was finished eating.

Eventually the two men died. The rich man's spirit went to a place of burning flames. When he looked far, far away, he could see Lazarus with all the angels in heaven. The rich man cried out to the angels, saying, "Please send Lazarus to me with a drop of water to cool my thirsty tongue."

But the answer came back, "Lazarus cannot cross the great gap between you and him. You had only good things in your life, where Lazarus lived with nothing but pain." For his selfishness, the rich man was now being tormented, while Lazarus finally had comfort.

The rich man cried out, "Please, at least send him to my five brothers. Let Lazarus tell them what will happen to them if they don't repent and share their good things with those in need."

"No," the angel said, "your brothers have the scriptures and the living prophets to teach them."

"But surely," cried the rich man, "if Lazarus came back from the dead, they would listen to his warning."

But the angel knew that they would not listen, even with a miracle.

I don't need a miracle to make me be good. I just need to read my scriptures and follow the prophet. What are some things the prophet has told me to do? What are the things I might need to change so I can follow the prophet?

The Royal Marriage Feast (Luke 14:16–24; variation in Matthew 22:2–14)

A king planned a great celebration for when his son was married. He invited all his important friends to attend. When the day came for the feast, the king sent a messenger to remind the guests to come. One by one, all the guests gave excuses, saying they were too busy to come.

The king was angry. He had planned this great party for his son, and no one was coming. He said his important friends had lost their chance to come. They were no longer welcome.

So he sent more messengers out into the kingdom to gather other guests to fill the halls, eat the food, and help to honor the occasion of the prince's marriage.

The people came. These people weren't beautiful, and they didn't have much money. Some of them weren't even good people at first. But they listened to the king's commands and they came.

The prophets are God's messengers. If I listen to the prophets and obey the commandments, I will be able to return to live with Heavenly Father and Jesus after I die. What are some of the things the prophets have asked me to do in these latter days?

Jesus Teaches Me to Be Kind to Others

The Good Samaritan (Luke 10:30–37)

A man was robbed while traveling. Thieves took his money and his clothes and hurt him so badly he couldn't stand. Then they left him lying in the road.

The first to pass by was a priest. He saw the injured man, but looked away, and moved to the other side of the road. Then came a Levite, a man from the church. But he didn't stop to help either.

Finally came a Samaritan. He wasn't from the same church; he wasn't even from the same country. But he stopped to help. The Samaritan went to the man in the road, cleaned his wounds, and gave him some water.

Then he picked up the man and set him on the Samaritan's donkey. He walked while the injured man rode. When they arrived at an inn, the Samaritan got a room for the man and took care of him.

The Samaritan had to continue on his own trip the next day. But before he left, he gave the innkeeper money to take care of the injured man. He also promised to return and pay any extra that was needed.

Each person is a child of God, and He loves all of us. If I see someone who needs my help, Heavenly Father would want me to stop and do something. I can be a friend to someone who doesn't have any friends. I can invite someone to listen to the missionaries. I know that Jesus wants me to be kind to others.

The Unmerciful Servant (Matthew 18:23–35)

A king brought together all of the people who owed him money. One man owed him ten thousand talents. When asked to pay back the debt, the man had nowhere near that amount of money.

The king said, "Then I will take everything you have, and you will go to jail until I have my money back."

The man fell to his knees and cried, "Please be patient with me. I'll work hard and pay you back everything, I promise."

The king was so moved by the man's request, he said, "It's all right. I forgive the debt. You don't have to pay back any of it."

Later, that same man went to one of his friends who owed him a hundred pence. It was just a small debt, but the man refused to listen to his friend's cries for more time. Instead, he sent his friend to prison.

When the king learned what the ungrateful man had done, he was angry. "I forgave your debt—ten thousand talents—because you asked me to. But you cannot forgive a mere hundred pence from one of your friends?" Then the king took all of the man's things and sold them. He sent the wicked man to prison until he could pay back all ten thousand talents that he owed.

🕭 *Jesus has given me everything. I could never pay Him back, but He has forgiven me. Because Jesus has forgiven my faults and mistakes, I need to forgive others. Is there someone I need to forgive?*

The Sheep and Goats (Matthew 25:31–46)

When Jesus comes again, all the people who have ever lived on earth will come to Him. Just as a shepherd divides his sheep from goats, putting the sheep on the right and goats on the left, Jesus will divide the people. He will place the good people to the right, and the bad, on the left.

Jesus will turn to those on His right and say, "Come with me. It is time for you to inherit the kingdom that I have prepared for you. You have earned it. I was hungry and you gave me meat. I was thirsty and you brought me water. I was alone and you became my friend. I was cold and you gave me warm clothes. I was sick in bed and you visited me."

And the good people will say, "Jesus, this is the first time we've seen you. So how can you say we did all those things for you?"

Jesus will explain, "When you did these things for others it was as though you did them for me."

Then Jesus will turn to those on His left and say, "Go now. You are not welcome here. I was hungry and thirsty, and you gave me nothing. I was alone, and you turned away from me. I was cold, and you gave me no clothes. I was sick, and you left me alone."

And the bad people will say, "Jesus, we've never even seen you before. How can you say we did such terrible things to you?"

Jesus will say, "When you would not help my brothers in need, you did not help me."

I want to be with Jesus, and so I know I must take care of others who need my help. What can I do to serve others?

Jesus Teaches Me to Pray

The Friend at Midnight (Luke 11:5–8)

In the middle of the night, a man woke to a knock on his door. It was a friend of his, asking for bread. The friend had some unexpected company and didn't have enough food to share with them.

Now, the man was very tired, and his wife and children were all sleeping. He didn't want to get up and get the bread, but he did. Because his friend asked for help, he could not refuse.

Heavenly Father loves me, and He wants to bless me. I need to remember to pray to Him when I need help or am lonely or frightened. What are some of the things I can ask for in my prayers?

The Selfish Judge (Luke 18:1–8)

There once was a judge who was very selfish. He didn't care about what God said was right, and he didn't care about the people in his city.

One day a widow came to him, asking for help to keep some men away who were being mean to her. The judge decided that would be too much work, so at first he refused to help her.

But the women kept coming in to ask for help. She came so many times that it began to annoy the judge. Finally he decided he would help her, just so he wouldn't have to hear her complain anymore.

If even that selfish judge helped the woman because she asked him to, then God will certainly help me if I ask Him. Do I need to pray more often?

Jesus Teaches Me to Repent

The Two Sons (Matthew 21:28–32)

A man had two sons. One day he asked them to help work on the farm. The first son said no, but later felt sorry. So he went and worked in the fields. The second son said that he would go, but instead busied himself with other things and never did help.

Even when I make a mistake or fail, Jesus is always willing to give me another chance. What I say I'll do is not as important as what I actually do. Is there anything I should do that I haven't done yet?

The Lost Sheep (Luke 15:4–7)

A shepherd had a hundred sheep. When he discovered that one had wandered off, he left the ninety-nine other sheep and set out to find the lost one. When he finally found it, he carried it home on his shoulders. Then he called all his friends together to celebrate finding his lost sheep.

Each of God's children is special to Him. Jesus loves me even when I make mistakes. When I repent of bad things I've done and say I am sorry, He is happy that I have returned to Him. Do I need to repent of anything today?

The Lost Piece of Silver (Luke 15:8–10)

A woman had ten pieces of silver. One day she counted them and found there were only nine. So she lit a candle, swept the house, and looked everywhere until she found it. When she found it, she ran to tell her friends and neighbors how happy she was to have found the missing piece.

I am special and loved by Jesus. He wants me to choose the right, but if I repent after I make a mistake, it makes Him especially happy. How can I bring my life closer to what it should be?

The Prodigal Son (Luke 15:11–32)

A man had two sons. The youngest son asked his father for his part of the inheritance. So the man divided everything he had and gave half of it to the younger son.

The boy took the money and went far away. He wanted to enjoy himself, so whenever he saw something he wanted, he would buy it. Soon his money ran out.

It happened that there was a famine in the land. Food was hard to find and very expensive. The boy needed to work just to earn money for food. He found work feeding pigs. The work was hard, and sometimes he even wished that he could eat some of the pig's food. But there was no food for him.

He thought of his family. He remembered that there was always plenty for everyone. Even the people who worked for his father always had more than enough to eat. So he decided to return to his father's house and ask to be a servant.

When the boy returned home, his father came running to him. He hugged the boy and gave him a new coat and shoes. The boy tried to explain that he only wanted to work, but the father wouldn't listen. He had a special dinner made to celebrate his son's return.

When the older son saw the preparations for the dinner and found out it was for his younger brother, he was angry. After all, he had stayed with his father and been good, doing everything just as he should. But he never got a big party for all his hard work.

His father agreed. It was true that the older son had always stayed with the family, and for that, he would inherit everything his father had. But they needed to celebrate the return of the younger son. He had been gone for so long, and the family could finally be together again.

Heavenly Father is watching and waiting for me to return to Him. Am I living the way I should? Do I need to repent? I want to feel the love of Jesus and of my Father in heaven.

Jesus Teaches Me to Choose the Right

The Gospel Net (Matthew 13:47–50)

Some fishermen threw their net out into the water. The net caught all different kinds of fish, and when it was full, the fishermen brought the net back to the shore. There they sorted through the fish. They kept all the fish that were good for eating but threw the bad fish away.

There are all kinds of people on earth, and on Judgment Day, Jesus will decide who is worthy to live with Him and with Heavenly Father. If I keep the commandments, I will be one of the chosen ones. What are some of the commandments I must keep to be worthy?

The Wheat and the Tares (Matthew 13:24–30)

A farmer planted good wheat in his fields. While he slept, someone played a mean trick on him and planted tares—poisonous weeds—in with the wheat seeds. The wheat started to grow but so did the tares.

The workers on the farm wondered where the tares came from, since they had used good seed. The farmer knew someone bad must have done it.

The workers asked the farmer if he wanted them to pull out the tares. But the farmer knew that would pull out the good wheat also. So he let the wheat and the tares grow up together.

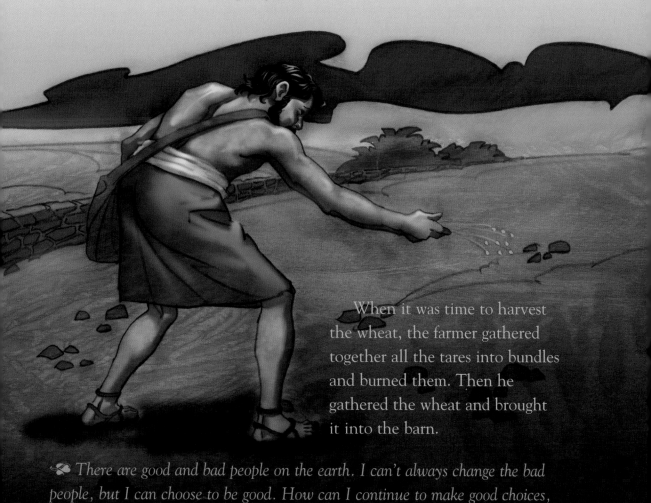

When it was time to harvest the wheat, the farmer gathered together all the tares into bundles and burned them. Then he gathered the wheat and brought it into the barn.

There are good and bad people on the earth. I can't always change the bad people, but I can choose to be good. How can I continue to make good choices,

Jesus Teaches Me to Watch and Prepare for When He Comes Again

The Tower (Luke 14:28–30)

Before building a tower, it is important to sit down and figure out how much it will cost to build. If a builder forgets to check the costs, he may find himself with just the foundation of a tower, but not have the money to finish it. The unfinished tower would mock him by sitting there, incomplete, reminding him of his failure and showing his weakness to the entire world.

When I choose to follow Jesus, I choose to follow Him for always. I must live each day preparing for when He comes again. Am I prepared to spend my whole life helping to build the Kingdom of God?

The Seed Growing Secretly (Mark 4:26–29)

A gardener takes a seed and plants it in the ground. He waters it and waits for it to grow. It takes a long time, and for a while it seems as though nothing is happening. Then one day he looks and sees a tiny green stem, where before there was only dirt.

The plant grows and bears fruit. The gardener doesn't know everything about how the plant grows, but he can see that it is growing. And when he sees that the fruit is ripe, he knows it is time to harvest.

Nobody knows exactly when Jesus will come again. But I know He will come and that there will be signs to let me know when He is coming. What are the signs I need to watch for?

The Ten Virgins (Matthew 25:1–13)

There was a great marriage planned. Ten women took their lamps and went to meet the bridegroom. Five were foolish. They brought their lamps, but only with whatever oil was already in them. Five were wise, bringing along extra oil to refill their lamps.

The bridegroom took a long time before coming, and the ten women fell asleep while they waited. At midnight, the women were called out to meet the bridegroom.

The five foolish women awoke and saw their lamps had gone out. They asked the others to share their oil. But the wise women had brought only enough for themselves. If they tried to share, all their lights might go out.

So the foolish women had to rush to buy more oil for their lamps. While they were gone, the bridegroom came. The five wise women went with him to the marriage, and the door was shut.

Later, the others came and knocked on the door. They cried, "Let us in!"

But the answer came, "I don't know you." So the five foolish women were left out in the night because they were not prepared.

I don't want to be left out when Jesus comes, so I will prepare myself. What are some things that I can do now so that I will be ready when He comes again?

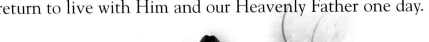

Jesus teaches me many wonderful things. He teaches me about our Father in Heaven. He teaches me how to have the peace that comes from choosing the right. And the greatest thing Jesus teaches me is that if I do my very best to listen and obey, I can return to live with Him and our Heavenly Father one day.

The Author

Randy-Lynne Wach received her bachelor's degree in English from Brigham Young University. Since then, she has studied a variety of topics, including writing, art, music, and dance. She now lives in northern Indiana with her husband, Terry, and their three daughters.

The Illustrator

Jerry Harston holds a degree in graphic design and has illustrated more than thirty children's books. He has received many honors for his art, and his clients include numerous Fortune 500 corporations. Jerry and his wife, Libby, live in Sandy, Utah. Their six children and sixteen grandchildren serve as excellent critics for his illustrations.